Hey Kids! Let's Visit Paris France

Teresa Mills

Life Experiences Publishing

Bluff City, Tennessee

Teresa Mills/Life Experiences Publishing
PO Box 53
Bluff City, TN 37618
www.kid-friendly-family-vacations.com

Book Layout © 2014 BookDesignTemplates.com

Hey Kids! Let's Visit Paris France/Teresa Mills -- 1st ed.
ISBN - 978-1-946049-03-2

Contents

Preface

Welcome

Like so many other places that you can visit, there are just so many things to do and see in Paris!

Paris, France, has two nicknames: the City of Light and the City of Love. It is called the City of Light for two different reasons—because of its role in the Age of Enlightenment (Age of Reason) and because it was one of the first European Cities to have gas street lights. The nickname City of Love comes from the fact that each year millions of people come to Paris for the romantic charm of the city.

This book is written as a fun fact guide about several Paris attractions and sites. The book includes some history interspersed with fun facts about things to do in the city. Parents can either read the book with their children or have their children read it themselves.

You can visit Paris, France, right from your own home with this book! You can enjoy this book whether you are preparing for a vacation with the family and want to learn more about the city or just wanting to learn a little more about Paris.

When you take your family trip to Paris, I have a free gift to help you plan! Go to this link to receive your gift:

http://kid-friendly-family-vacations.com/parisattractions

Also, take advantage of our companion activity and coloring books to complement this book… available as a set and separately.

https://kid-friendly-family-vacations.com/parispkg

When you have completed this book, I invite you to enjoy the other books in the series. We visit Washington DC, a Cruise Ship, New York City, San Francisco, Savannah Georgia, London England, and Charleston South Carolina.

Enjoy!
Teresa Mills

Introduction

A Little About Paris France

Paris is most famous for the romantic feel of its surroundings, but that's only a small part of this amazing city. Paris is the home of many famous museums and monuments. Paris is also home to almost three hundred thousand dogs—yep, dogs!

Paris is called the Garden of France because it has so many parks and gardens. Paris is a very clean city, and its parks and gardens are all very well maintained!

Like to read? Paris has a total of 830 libraries!

There are many things to do and see in Paris. It is definitely a place to soak in history!

So, are you ready?
Let's visit Paris, France!

Musee d'Orsay

Musée d'Orsay, or Orsay Museum in English, is an art museum in Paris. It was established in 1986 by François Mitterrand. Filled mostly with French art from the nineteenth century, Musée d'Orsay is considered to be a cultural historic site, housing works from famous artists such as Monet and Van Gogh. You will see different kinds of art, such as paintings, photography, architecture, decorative arts, and even furniture.

Musée d'Orsay is one of the biggest art museums in Europe. It holds the record for the largest collection of impressionist and post-impressionist paintings in the world. Van Gogh's works, which can be found in the museum, are a good example of impressionist paintings.

Several famous paintings can be found in the museum, such as William-Adolphe Bouguereau's

The Birth of Venus and Vincent van Gogh's *Starry Night over the Rhône*. Sculptures from major sculptors such as Pierre-Jules Cavelier, Camille Claudel, and Auguste Rodin are also there.

An interesting thing about the museum is its building's long history. The museum was actually once a railway station and hotel called Gare d'Orsay, or Station of Orsay. The station was also used as a set for several films, a safe haven for the Renaud-Barrault Theatre Company. When it was no longer needed as a train station (due to its instability and unsuitability for longer trains), it was decided to demolish the station. The Directorate of the Museums of France then decided to turn the station into an art museum.

It took over half a year to bring in all two thousand or so paintings, six hundred sculptures, furniture, and other works. Then, the museum officially opened in December 1986. The museum hosts visitors from around the world.

The building itself, built in 1900, is classified as Beaux-Arts architecture, an academic and neo-classical architecture style. It is characterized by a flat roof, arches, two clock towers, and symmetry. Since it was once a railway station, the building is also long.

Elephant in front of Musee d'Orsay

Ranked third nationally, Musée d'Orsay is truly a cultural wonder, a reflection of the French passion for the arts.

Fun Facts about the Musée d'Orsay

- More than ninety million people have already visited the museum. That's ninety million!

- The museum was once a railway station.

- Before it became a railway station, and later a museum, it was originally built as the Supreme Court!

2

Eiffel Tower

The Eiffel Tower is a lattice tower made of twisted iron that can be found in Champ de Mars, a large grassy field in Paris. The tower is named after Gustave Eiffel, the engineer whose firm designed and erected the tower. The construction of the tower began in 1887 and ended in 1889 as the main symbol for the 1889 World Fair, a celebration of the French Revolution.

Though its design was initially criticized by many artists and intellectuals of France, it has become a cultural icon of the country, as well as one of the most well-known structures in the world. It is also the most frequently visited paid monument in the world. In fact, over 6.9 million people visit the tower annually.

The tower is the tallest structure in Paris—it is 1,063 feet (324 meters) tall, or the same height as a building with eighty-one floors. In France, it is second only to the Millau Viaduct in height.

The tower has three levels for visitors. Restaurants can be found on the first and second levels, while the third level serves as an observation deck.

An interesting fact about the tower is that Gustave Eiffel himself engraved on the tower the names of seventy-two French engineers, scientists, and mathematicians as a symbol of recognition for their contributions in building the tower.

The tower weighs, in total, 10,100 tons. It is painted in three shades, darkest at the bottom and lightest at the top. This was done to complement the Parisian sky. To prevent the tower from rusting, sixty tons of paint are applied every seven years.

In addition to being an observation tower and tourist attraction, the tower is also used to make radio transmissions. Television antennas are installed on the tower, though analog television signals from the tower ceased transmission on March 8, 2011.

Eiffel Tower

Known worldwide as a symbol of love, the Eiffel Tower is a common destination for honeymooners and couples. This would only make sense, as the Eiffel Tower was built in Paris, the city of love. In addition to that, it is also widely known as an architectural wonder. In fact, around twenty-five thousand people, on average, visit the tower every single day, and many more go to the Champ de Mars to get a view of the tower from a distance.

Fun Facts about the Eiffel Tower

- The Eiffel Tower is nicknamed the Iron Lady (La Dame de Fer) because it's made mostly of iron.

- The tower can shrink and grow by as much as six inches? How? When the sun is out, the tower grows because the metal expands.

- The tower is repainted every seven years. It takes 60 tons of paint.

- There are 7 million visitors to the tower every year.

3

Musée du Louvre

Musée du Louvre, or Museum of Louvre, is a museum in Paris. The museum, also the central landmark of the city of Paris, holds the record as the world's largest museum and is considered a historic monument of France. Around twenty-eight thousand items, from prehistoric times to the twenty-first century, are on exhibit, in an area of over 782,910 square feet.

Housed in Louvre Palace, the museum was originally a fortress built during the time of Philip II in the late twelfth century. After the loss of its defensive function because of the city's urban expansion, it was converted into the main residence for French kings. Then it was a place to showcase the royal collection, and finally, since 1692 it has been occupied by Académie des Inscriptions et Belles Lettres and Académie Royale de Peinture et de Sculpture, where they held the first series of salons. Though the Louvre has remained with the Académie for over one hundred years, during the French Revolution it was decreed that the Louvre be used to display the country's national treasures and masterpieces.

Musée du Louvre

The Louvre's most popular attraction is one of the world's most famous paintings—Leonardo Da Vinci's *Mona Lisa*. Other famous works of art found in the museum include Alexandros of Antioch's *Venus de Milo*, Michelangelo's *Dying Slave*, and Eugène Delacroix's *Liberty Leading the People*.

The museum itself contains more than 380,000 objects and 35,000 works of art, spanning sculptures, paintings, drawings, archaeological finds, and objets d'art (works of art).

The Louvre is the second most visited museum in the world. It welcomes over 7.4 million visitors a year. The museum hosts over fifteen thousand visitors a day, 65 percent of which are foreign tourists.

The museum has eight curatorial departments with over 652,000 square feet dedicated to the permanent collection of exhibits. These curatorial departments include Egyptian antiquities, Near Eastern antiquities, Roman, Greek, and Etruscan art, Islamic art, sculptures, decorative art, paintings, and prints and drawings.

Another interesting feature of the Louvre Museum is its main entrance, the Louvre Pyramid, which has become a landmark of the city of Paris. The structure consists of glass panes and metal poles, which earned the structure the nickname the Glass Pyramid.

Established in 1793, the museum is rightfully ranked first nationally and second globally. The Musée du Louvre is truly a grandiose setting, the pride of France, and a reflection of the country's appreciation for history and the arts.

Fun Facts about the Musée du Louvre

- Did you know that Leonardo da Vinci's *Mona Lisa* is not really as big as many people think? With its size of twenty-one by thirty inches, it is just a bit bigger than a sheet of poster board.

- The Louvre is the largest museum in the world. So large that it would be impossible to see everything in one visit.

- The museum is haunted by a mummy named Belphegor.

- The glass pyramid is 21 meters tall.

4

Notre Dame Cathedral

The Notre Dame Cathedral is a prime example of French Gothic sculpture, architecture, and stained glass. It's also France's most popular monument, with over thirteen million visitors annually. Dedicated to the Virgin Mary, it's also actively used as a Catholic church. As Catholicism's main symbol in France, the cathedral hosts pilgrimages and nationally important religious events.

The cathedral has had a tumultuous history, with the building standing on the site of the first Christian church in Paris. It's also historically significant as Napoleon Bonaparte was crowned Emperor here on December 2, 1804. A mass to celebrate Paris's liberation took place on August 26, 1944.

As an artistic masterpiece and one of early Gothic architecture's most famous examples, a trip to

Notre Dame Cathedral

Paris is not complete without a visit to Notre Dame Cathedral. Each part of the cathedral is hailed an artistic wonder.

The west front features the South Tower, which holds the thirteen-ton bell named Emmanuel. The Grand Gallery contains the legendary yet functional gargoyles. The King's Gallery is a line of twenty-eight statues featuring the kings of Israel and Judah.

In addition to the portals, the stained glass windows are important examples of thirteenth-century art. Of interest are the west rose window, the south rose window, and the north rose window.

Fun Facts about Notre Dame Cathedral

- Gargoyles were built to scare evil spirits away and remind sinners of the demons waiting for them in hell. However, did you know that gargoyles are also used in a practical sense? As rain gutters! Even today, water from the roof flows along each gargoyle's grooved back, until their mouths spew out water, away from the building to keep the cathedral's foundations solid and dry.

- An interesting statue on the cathedral's western façade's left-hand doorway is the statue of a beheaded Saint Denis. Legend says that the Romans, in 250 AD, caught the saint preaching Christianity and ordered that he be killed at Montmartre. He was beheaded halfway up the hill. According to legend, the saint's headless body stands up, picks up its head, and walks for a few miles—while the head continued to preach about Christianity. Definitely spooky!

- The cathedral has undergone periods of restoration and destruction. In the sixteenth century, the French king and the Huguenots changed the cathedral's appearance. The cathedral, during the French Revolution, was used to store food, and many of the statues' heads were removed. The damage has since been reversed, and more additions have been built. The 1991–2010 restoration saw the cleaning and preservation of the façade and sculptures.

- Notre Dame's organs, the cathedral's centerpiece, have been added over the years. The organs and the bells are reason enough to visit the cathedral. The main bell, located in the South Tower, weighs more than thirteen tons. Traditionally rung by hand, electric motors were installed during the twentieth century to ring the bells.

5

Sainte-Chapelle

What makes the Sainte-Chapelle in Paris, so impressive, considering its artistic and architectural intricacy, is that it was built in only seven years. The sumptuous yet intimate chapel was built within the Parisian royal residence—the Palais de la Cité—by Louis IX. Today, the UNESCO-designated World Heritage site is one of Rayonnant architecture's best examples.

The chapel is considered a forerunner of structures mostly made of glass. It was built six hundred years prior to the Crystal Palace and eight hundred years prior to the glass pyramid of the Louvre. It clearly shows how radically the medieval master masons rethought architecture.

Sainte-Chapelle

In addition to housing the holiest of relics, the chapel was vital for the king's cultural and political ambitions to be western Christendom's central monarch. During the time of the chapel's construction, the Holy Roman Empire was in disarray and the Constantinople imperial throne was occupied by the Count of Flanders. King Louis IX was canonized by the Catholic Church as a saint. He became Saint Louis.

In June 1940, Adolf Hitler visited the chapel during his one trip to Paris. Sainte-Chapelle now draws nine hundred thousand visitors annually. Since the 1970s, the chapel has been undergoing restoration. The elements of weather, air pollution, and the number of visitors were causing damage to the windows.

Fun Facts about Sainte-Chapelle

- The chapel's highlight is its stained glass windows, which were restored during the nineteenth century. They tell the tale of humankind from the Creation to the world's Redemption through Jesus Christ. The windows encompass glass with a 6,458-square-foot area, with two-thirds of the glass still original. Lancets divide the windows. One should read them left to right and from bottom to top.

- Sainte-Chapelle is thirty-six meters long, seventeen meters wide, and 42.5 meters high. Its exterior is typical of Rayonnant architecture, which is characterized by deep, pinnacle-surmounted buttresses, crocket gables around the roof, and bar-tracery-divided windows.

- The slate roof is marked by the thirty-three-meter-high cedar wood spire, a fine nineteenth-century masterpiece, which is a replica of the fifteenth-century spire. A string course marks the internal division into the lower and upper chapels. The lower walls are pierced by smaller spherical triangular-shaped windows.

- The upper chapel is usually reserved for the king, his family, and close friends. It's also used to display religious relics, especially the Passion relics, including the Crown of Thorns. Such relics catapulted France into Latin Christendom's forefront. The lower chapel is dedicated to Mother Mary.

6

Luxembourg Gardens

The Italian Baroque-style Luxembourg Gardens in Paris is popular and has been considered a quintessential Parisian space. The gardens are dominated by a parterre, which is a formal garden arranged in geometrical patterns. To the gardens' southwest are a puppet theater as well as pear and apple orchards.

One of the Luxembourg Gardens' most appealing attributes is that it's relaxing. Despite the grandness of the gardens, ordinary people feel comfortable eating lunch, walking around, and escaping the heat in the Medici Fountain's shadows.

In the gardens, visitors can freely sit, read, play chess, daydream, enjoy Turkish coffee in a café, or drink wine at the music kiosk. Between the

French Garden and the Rue Guynemer, visitors can play tennis and other sports.

The gardens also house the Musée du Luxembourg, which holds art exhibitions. Around the rear of the museum, in the palace orangery, orange and lemon trees, grenadiers, oleanders, and palms provide shelter from the cold.

The Duke of Luxembourg was the gardens' original owner, before it was bought in 1612 by Marie de' Medici. Originally, the gardens occupied an area of eight hectares. However, Medici bought more land and expanded the gardens considerably.

Medici assigned the landscaping to Jacques Boyceau de la Barauderie, who designed the garden with rectangular flower beds fronting the palace. The gardens are regular features in French literature. The most famous entry is in Victor Hugo's *Les Miserables* during the scene when Cosette and Marius first meet.

Luxembourg Gardens

Fun Facts about the Luxembourg Gardens

- Spanning a humongous area of twenty-three hectares, the Luxembourg Gardens is Paris's second largest park. It has a total of 106 statues that feature famous people like Flaubert, Beethoven, Frederic Chopin, and Baudelaire, among others. There are also Greek mythology statues, animal statues, and a small Statue of Liberty.

- The gardens serve as the Palais du Luxembourg backdrop. The palace was built in the 1620s for Henri IV's consort, Marie de Medici, to satisfy her longing for Florence's Pitti Palace, where she had lived as a child. East of the Palais du Luxembourg is the Italian-style Fontaine des Medici, which was built in 1630. As the palace now houses the Senate, people can wander through it and listen to Senate proceedings.

- Through the centuries, the gardens were neglected by French monarchs, and revitalization did not begin until after the end of the French Revolution. It was only during the nineteenth century that the gardens were enlarged and redeveloped under French architect Gabriel Davioud's supervision.

• Napoleon dedicated the gardens to Paris's children. Many of the city's residents spent their childhood prodding the sailboats on the Grand Bassin pond. They also rode on the merry-go-round (carousel) and ponies. The same activities are still being enjoyed, as are contemporary playgrounds and games and sporting events.

7

River Seine

The Seine River is one of the most famous waterways in France. It runs through several parts of the country. Its history is long and rich, as it is one of the most important rivers in France.

One of France's most important waterways

The Seine River is one of the most important bodies of water in France because of its crucial commercial use. The river has been used for centuries as a means to move cargo from one part of France to another. In fact, the river has served as an important commercial highway since the time of the Romans.

River Seine

Bridges everywhere

The Seine River bisects France's capital, Paris, into the River Droite, the Right Bank, and the River Gauche, the Left Bank. Paris has thirty-seven bridges inside its borders to allow its citizens to traverse the river. While there are plenty of bridges inside Paris, there are many more outside of its borders in various towns, villages, and cities.

In fact, the Seine River is crossed by one of France's most famous bridges, the Pont de Normandie. Pont de Normandie is a cable-stayed bridge that links Honfleur to Le Havre. At the time of its completion in 1995, Pont de Normandie was the longest bridge of its kind on the entire planet.

One of the most famous tourist attractions

The Seine River is one of the most famous tourist attractions in Paris. There are a lot of tour guides that make money showing off the wonderful views of the river from around the city.

Avoid drinking the water

There have been various times in the past when the sewage system of Paris could not keep up with all the waste. The Seine River has welcomed this excess waste several times in the past when the sewage was discharged to the river. While water quality is better now than before, it is still inadvisable to drink the water in Seine River.

Caused a great art migration

At times, rainfall has caused the river to overflow. It can overflow to the point where it can cause flooding in Paris. In 2003, around one hundred thousand pieces of art were moved from Paris to avoid potential destruction caused by a flood.

Fun Facts about the River Seine

- The Seine River is very famous for its romantic Bateaux Mouches, or sightseeing boats.

- The river's mouth is at least sixteen kilometers, or ten miles wide.

- It is the second longest river that flows entirely in France.

8

Basilique du Sacré-Cœur de Montmartre

The Sacré-Cœur Basilica (Basilica of the Sacred Heart) is a minor basilica and church located in Paris that is devoted to the Sacred Heart of Jesus. It is one of Paris's more famous landmarks and can be found at butte Montmartre's summit.

Built to commemorate a loss

In 1870, the French lost the Franco-Prussian War to the Germans. The people of France vowed to build a church if Paris remained unscathed during the Prussian War. Paris remained unharmed at the end of the war, so France constructed the Sacré-Cœur Basilica to commemorate the event.

Basilica of the Sacred Heart

One of the most fantastic views of Paris

Sacré-Cœur Basilica sits quite high in Paris. The Sacré-Cœur Basilica's top dome is open to the public for viewing. The flight of stairs that is used to access the top of the dome might be long, but it is worth the trek for the breathtaking view of Paris.

The Basilica's white color

The construction materials used to make Sacré-Cœur Basilica came from the Château-Landon quarries. The stone is calcite. Wet weather is what gives the stone of Sacré-Cœur Basilica its white appearance.

A Christian sanctuary

Sacré-Cœur Basilica is a chapel built to honor the first bishop of Paris, Saint Denis. The story goes that Saint Denis was beheaded in this location by the Romans. After being beheaded, the body of Saint Denis picked up his head and began to walk around while his head was delivering complete sermons. The body stopped abruptly and the point where he stopped is where Sacré-Cœur Basilica was built.

Worship before the construction of Sacré-Cœur Basilica

Before its construction, the site of Sacré-Cœur Basilica was supposedly a sacred site for Druids (priests, magicians, and soothsayers, in the ancient Celtic religion) to practice their worship. During the Roman era, temples were built and dedicated to the Roman gods Mercury and Mars.

Fun Facts about the Sacré-Cœur Basilica

- Did you know that Druids used to worship on the hill where the basilica stands? Likewise, the ancient Romans constructed temples for Mercury and Mars there.

- You can listen to live music on the steps of Sacré-Cœur as you enjoy the city view, especially on warm evenings.

- The stained glass windows in the basilica were destroyed in 1944. They were then replaced in 1946.

9

Arc de Triomphe

Without a doubt, the Arc de Triomphe is one of Paris's most famous attractions. It stands at the western-most point of the Avenue des Champs-Élysées.

Commissioned by Napoleon Bonaparte

The arc was commissioned by one of France's most noteworthy historical figures, Napoleon Bonaparte. Sadly, Napoleon Bonaparte would never get to see the completed monument since it was finished fifteen years after his death.

Napoleon commissioned the construction of the Arc de Triomphe in commemoration of the people who died fighting for France during the Napoleonic and French Revolutionary Wars. The outer and inner surfaces of the arch are inscribed with the names of the generals and all the major French victories.

Arc de Triomphe

Plane once flew right through the arch

The Arc de Triomphe is one of the widest arches in existence. To commemorate the end of World War I, Charles Godefroy flew a biplane through the Arc de Triomphe's main vault. It was even captured on a newsreel. A video of the event can be found on the internet.

One of the tallest of its kind in the world

At the time of its completion, the Arc de Triomphe was noted as the tallest arch in the world. It stood at a height of fifty meters, or 164 feet. It would be surpassed about a hundred years later in Mexico by the Monumento a la Revolución, which stands at a height of sixty-seven meters, or 220 feet.

Could have been an elephant

Before being dedicated as a site for the Arc de Triomphe, this location was almost dedicated to a gigantic elephant. Charles Ribart, a French architect, proposed that a giant three-story building in the shape of an elephant be erected at the site where the Arc de Triomphe stands today.

The Tomb of the Unknown Soldier

A tomb was built under the Arc de Triomphe. An eternal flame was then lit in honor of those who had died during the war. The tomb was visited by John and Jackie Kennedy. Inspired by the eternal flame, Jackie Kennedy had a similar one lit after US President John F. Kennedy was assassinated.

Fun Facts about the Arc de Triomphe

- Did you know that the Tomb of the Unknown Soldier represents 1.5 million soldiers who perished in World War I?

- Bet you didn't know that it used to be the largest triumphal arch in the world, but North Korea intentionally built a bigger one in 1982.

- The Eternal Flame has never been extinguished from the time it was first lit on November 11, 1923.

10

The Catacombs

When people think of Paris, most people see a beautiful city full of amazing landmarks that are testaments to human achievements in the arts, architecture, and engineering. Few people know, let alone think, about the Catacombs of Paris.

The Catacombs of Paris is a collection of ossuaries, sites that serve as the final resting place for human skeletons that can be found underneath the city of lights. Known officially as l'Ossuaire Municipal or Catacombes officiels, the Paris Catacombs is one of the most famous landmarks in Paris.

Here are a few fun and interesting facts about Paris's underground cemetery:

Holds remains of about six million people

There are many rough estimates as to the number of human remains that have been placed inside the Paris Catacombs. However, reasonable estimates put the number of human remains in the catacombs at around six million.

Entrance called the Gate of Hell

The entrance to one of the world's biggest cemeteries is named the Gate of Hell. Luckily it is not as hot as most people would imagine it to be down there.

Never completely mapped

It is illegal to enter the catacombs without permission from the local government. The reason for this is that the tunnels span more than two hundred kilometers (124.27 miles), making it extremely easy to get lost. Most of it has not been mapped.

The Catacombs

For all legal intents and purposes, a museum

Paris Musées is a public corporation tasked to handle the fourteen museums of Paris. As of 2013, the Paris Catacombs counts as one of the museums that this institution is meant to maintain and protect.

Airbnb's desire to let people stay a night for free

Airbnb held a competition that allowed winners to stay in the cemetery portions of the massive tunnel system. They were treated to a warm bed as well as a meal.

Paris catacombs' role in World War II

Germany occupied Paris during World War II. The French Resistance during the war used the tunnels as a way to get around the city and support their movement.

Romans' mining of the network for limestone and gypsum

The tunnels that make the catacombs are actually mining tunnels that trace all the way back to the time when the Romans occupied Paris. Limestone and gypsum were both mined here, most of which were used to construct the majority of the city's buildings.

Graffiti artists and art shows under the tunnels

Paris is home to a lot of artists, some of whom prefer to use walls as their canvases. The need to express their art has led some artists to go into the tunnels to spray paint on some of its sections. Not just that, but the tunnels of the Paris Catacombs are also famous for holding some clandestine art shows.

Movies

The catacombs not only is home to a ton of human skeletons but also serves as a home to a lot of lost loot. There is a police task force that patrols the tunnels to make sure that no one trespasses illegally. Once, the police found a secret cinema complete with an electric screen, seating carved from the walls of the tunnels, and even a bar.

Fun Facts about the Paris Catacombs

- This is scary but fun at the same time. In some rooms, you need to walk through piles of skeletons to pass through.

- King Charles hosted wild parties inside the Paris Catacombs.

- Sneaking down the unmapped areas of the catacombs can be dangerous! A lot of people get lost doing that.

11

Trocadéro

The Trocadéro is across the Seine River from the Eiffel Tower. The hill of Trocadéro is the hill of Chaillot, which was once a village.

Here are some of the interesting facts:

Named after a huge battle

The Trocadéro actually takes its name from a famous battle fought in 1823, the Battle of Trocadéro. It was a battle fought when the French invaded Spain to fight its army and restore King Ferdinand VII's absolute rule.

King Ferdinand VII faced a rebellion for his refusal to adopt a constitutional monarchy. The powers of Europe convened, and it was through the Congress of Verona that France was authorized to help the deposed monarch of Spain reestablish his rule.

Trocadéro

To commemorate this victory, the Duke of Angoulême, Louis Antoine, was given the title Prince of Trocadéro. The Place of Trocadéro itself was located at the outskirts of the then expanding Paris.

Best place for a selfie

Trocadéro itself is across the Seine River from the Eiffel Tower. Its location makes it an ideal place to take a picture or a selfie with one of Paris's most famous, if not the most famous, landmark, the Eiffel Tower.

A wonderful place for nature lovers

Jardins du Trocadéro is a wonderful garden covering ten thousand square meters (11,960 square yards). The garden was built in 1937 for the International Exposition. At the center of this garden is the Warsaw fountain. The fountain is composed of twenty water cannons that serve as the centerpiece of Jardins du Trocadéro.

Palais de Chaillot

The International Exposition of 1937 saw the demolition of Palais du Trocadéro. It was then replaced by the Palais de Chaillot, which is the palace that now sits atop the hill. Palais de Chaillot has two wings that form a massive arc. In fact, most of Palais de Chaillot was built on the foundation laid down by Palais du Trocadéro.

Palais de Chaillot is also home to several gilded figures, which were made by some of France's most accomplished artists, such as Marcel Gimond, Alexandre Descatoire, Robert Couturier, and many others.

Home to Several Museums

In addition to the sculptures, the size of Palais de Chaillot also allows it to house several of Paris's museums and a theater. The Musée de l'Homme (ethnology), the Musée national de la Marine (naval museum), Musée national des Monuments Français, Cité de l'Architecture et du Patrimoine (Architecture and Heritage City), as well as the Théâtre national de Chaillot can be found in Palais de Chaillot.

Fun Facts about the Trocadéro

- If you tour Paris, you will most likely take a selfie on this hill, which is where you can find the most magnificent landmarks and most picturesque locations in Paris.

- Ironically, Trocadéro was named after a bloody battle.

- There is an aquarium with over 43 tanks at the Trocadéro.

12

Champs-Élysées

The Avenue des Champs-Élysées is one of the most famous streets in France and probably the world. The eighth arrondissement (administrative district) of Paris is home to Champs-Élysées. You can't say that you've completely toured Paris until you have walked along this avenue.

Here are a few interesting facts about Champs-Élysées:

Champs-Élysées, before becoming what it is today, used to be kitchen gardens and fields. It was then laid out by André Le Nôtre in 1667 to serve as an extension for the Tuileries Garden. This garden extension would not take on its present name until 1709.

Champs-Élysées

By the eighteenth century, Champs-Élysées had become the fashionable avenue that it is known today. Some of the grandest mansions of the nobility could be found along this street. Perhaps the most well-known home was the Élysée Palace, which served as home for the presidents of France at the time of the Third French Republic.

Champs-Élysées has also seen its fair share of military parades. German armies paraded through this street twice, once in 1871 when Kaiser Wilhelm I and his troops entered Paris victoriously and once more in 1940 to commemorate the Fall of France. Both US and French armed forces marched through this street during the end of both World War I and World War II.

Heaven on earth

Champs-Élysées is French for Elysian Fields. Elysium, or the Elysian Fields, is a realm in Greek Mythology. It was a place where the gods of the Greek pantheon as well as their heroes resided. As the story went, only those who lived a moral and good life were allowed to enter Elysium in the afterlife. To put it simply, it is the equivalent of heaven. To call the street Champs-Élysées is like saying that it is like a slice of heaven on earth.

A meeting point for the brilliant

The French are sometimes stereotypically portrayed in the media as being the intellectual type—the type of people who spend most of their afternoons and evenings sipping well-brewed coffee in a café while discussing intellectual topics.

What most people do not know is that these French intellectuals used to call Champs-Élysées their home. That's right. When media portrays an elegant and luxurious French café, it is most probably inspired by the intellectuals (scientists and artists) who gathered on Champs-Élysées during its glory days.

Shops and boutiques

In addition to French cafés, the street is also famous for being home to some of the best stores in Paris. Champs-Élysées was and still is one of the most famous locations for upscale shopping in the world. It serves as a home to several luxury brands, such as Lacoste, Lancel, Louis Vuitton, Hugo Boss, and many more.

The most exclusive hotel in Paris

Hôtel de Crillon is considered by many to be the most exclusive place to stay in Paris. It is right in front of the American embassy and is the hotel where King Louis XVI met with Benjamin Franklin to sign a treaty to recognize the independence of the United States.

Fun Facts about Champs-Élysées

- Did you know that the largest military parade in the whole of Europe passes along Champs-Élysées? It happens each year on Bastille Day and is attended by the French president.

- Champs-Élysées is only the second most expensive real estate strip in Europe. Do you know which is the most expensive? It's Bond Street in London.

- The avenue is considered one of the most beautiful and luxurious streets in the entire world.

13

Versailles

Few places embody the idea of French grandeur and beauty more than Château de Versailles. The château started off as a hunting lodge for King Louis XIV's father. At some point during his reign, King Louis XIV moved his court from Paris to Versailles. The kings of France would rule and hold court here until the French Revolution.

Château de Versailles is about sixty miles from Paris, a really good option for a day trip while visiting Paris!

Originally nothing more than a hunter's retreat

Château de Versailles was not always the grand palace that it is today. When first built, Château

de Versailles was built as King Louis XIII's hunting lodge in 1623. Louis the XIV was responsible
for making Château de Versailles what it is today.

Versailles

Château de Versailles is massive in both size and
numbers. It covers 721,182 square feet, or sixty-
thousand square meters, has two thousand windows, seven hundred rooms, sixty-seven
staircases, and 1,250 fireplaces.

A room of reflection

Out of the seven hundred rooms, perhaps the
most famous one of all is the world-renowned
Hall of Mirrors. The hall houses 357 mirrors and

serves as the central gallery of Château de Versailles. King Louis XIV would walk daily from his apartment, through the Hall of Mirrors, to the chapel. It was here that most courtiers would try to get an invitation from King Louis XIV.

A bright wonder

The reason why Château de Versailles has so many mirrors and chandeliers was because palace officials wanted to perfect the art of lighting. Remember, Château de Versailles was made long before the light bulb. They redefined indoor lighting by extensive use of mirrors and chandeliers that reflected the light from some twenty thousand candles.

Built from the king's purse

Initially, Château de Versailles was meant to be King Louis XIV's home away from the palace. During the early years, Château de Versailles's construction and expansion were funded by the king's private coffers. It was mostly funded from the revenue King Louis XIV received from New France, modern-day Canada. New France was a part of Canada but considered to be a private possession of the king.

A grand showcase of French craft and mercantilism

King Louis XIV began construction campaigns to expand the château, so he needed more money. Jean-Baptiste Colbert, as finance minister, had the idea to make Château de Versailles a showcase for French craft. Much of Château de Versailles's decorations, furniture, and silverware were all made in France.

Colbert's idea met success as Château de Versailles was admired, and even copied, by several of Europe's kingdoms.

Fun Facts about Château de Versailles

- Upon completion, Chateau de Versailles could accommodate as many as five thousand people.

- With over seven hundred rooms, 1,250 fireplaces, sixty-seven staircases, two thousand windows and over 1,800 acres of park area, the château is considered one of the largest palaces in the whole world.

- In 1789, townspeople were starving. Led by women, they marched to the palace to demand for bread.

14

Paris Bike Tours

Paris is a great place to tour on a bike. It's not surprising that bike tours in Paris are popular as they allow you to cover a large area without having to battle your way through traffic.

Bike Share System

Fortunately, finding a bike in Paris is easy, thanks to Vélib', which is a bike share system. This lets you easily find a bike around the city. The bike share is available twenty-four hours a day—take a bike, and then return it. If you are interested in this self-service type of bike tour, check into the Vélib' pass.

There are several Tour Companies that offer guided bike tours as well:

Fat Tire Tours—Paris Day Bike Tour

See the famous sites, hear fun and interesting stories, and learn about the great city of Paris. Lunch at a local cafe is on the tour, and you'll receive lots of personalized attention from the tour guides.

Blue Fox Travel - Blue Bike Tours

Blue Bike Tours has two different bike tours of Paris to choose from. The Best of Paris Bike Tour offers the best of Paris in just four hours. You will see the sites and hear fun historical facts and hear stories that you wouldn't normally hear about each museum or monument. The Hidden Paris Bike Tour gives you a truly local Paris experience. This is sort of an off-the-beaten-path tour of Paris.

Bike About Tours

Bike About Tours gives you the insider's view of Paris—insider info, local secrets. Bike About Tours sticks with the backstreets and local neighborhoods to give tourists a unique view of the city.

Paris by Bike

Paris by bike is one of the best ways to visit the city. This tour company specializes in hidden passageways, food tasting, and out-of-the-ordinary visits to museums and monuments.

I hope you enjoyed visiting Paris. Now let's head east across the English Channel to London, England where we will learn about the iconic red phone booths!

https://kid-friendly-family-vacations.com/booktour-visitlondon

----

Sign up for my newsletter for all upcoming updates as well as some free gifts.

https://kid-friendly-family-vacations.com/parisattractions

Rather head to the USA? Hop a flight to New York City to find out about a building that looks like an iron and a beach amusement park a short subway ride from downtown Manhattan!

https://kid-friendly-family-vacations.com/booktour-visitnyc

Learn more about the entire Hey Kids! Let's Visit series!

https://kid-friendly-family-vacations.com/booktour-series

Please leave a review to help others lean more about Paris whether traveling or learning from home.

https://kid-friendly-family-vacations.com/review-paris

MORE FROM KID FRIENDLY FAMILY VACATIONS

BOOKS

Books to help build your kids / grandkids life experiences through travel and learning

https://kid-friendly-family-vacations.com/books

COLORING AND ACTIVITY PAGKAGES

Coloring pages, activity books, printable travel journals, and more in our Etsy shop

https://kid-friendly-family-vacations.com/etsy

RESOURCES FOR TEACHERS

Resources for teachers on Teachers Pay Teachers

https://kid-friendly-family-vacations.com/tpt

It is our mission to help you build your children's and grand-children's life experiences through travel. Not just traveling with your kids... building their "Life Experiences"! Join our community here: https://kid-friendly-family-vacations.com/join

Acknowledgements

Proof-reading / Editing

Deb Hall – TheWriteInsight.com

Cover Photos

Arc de Triomphe – © gurgenb / deposit photos

Eiffel Tower - © encrier / deposit photos

Musee du Louvre - © richie0703 / deposit photos

River Seine from Eiffel Tower – © olgacov / deposit photos

The Catacombs - © bukki88 / deposit photos

Photos in Book

Musee d'Orsay - elephant statue - © bloodua / deposit photos

Eiffel Tower - © encrier / deposit photos

Musee du Louvre - © richie0703 / deposit photos

Notre Dame Cathedral – © Vichaya Kiatying-Angsulee / 123rf.com

Sainte-Chapelle - © zatletic/ deposit photos

Luxemburg Gardens – © Roman Milert / 123rf.com

River Seine from Eiffel Tower – © olgacov / deposit photos

Basilica of the Sacred Heart - © gornostaj / deposit photos

Arc de Triomphe – © gurgenb / deposit photos

The Catacombs - © bukki88 / deposit photos

Trocadero - © tanjakrstevska / deposit photos

Champs-Elysees - © Tupungato / deposit photos

Versailles - © fyletto / deposit photos

ABOUT THE AUTHOR

Teresa Mills is the best selling author of the "Hey Kids! Let's Visit..." Book Series for Kids!

Teresa's goal through her books and website is to help parents / grand-parents who want to build the life experiences of their children / grand-children through travel and learning activities.

She is an active mother and Mimi. She and her family love traveling in the USA, and internationally too! They love exploring new places, eating cool foods, and having yet another adventure as a family! With the Mills, it's all about traveling as family.

In addition to traveling, Teresa enjoys reading, hiking, biking, and helping others.

Join in the fun at http://kid-friendly-family-vacations.com

Made in the USA
Coppell, TX
14 November 2022

86380656R00046